Index

Title	Page
Pet details	2
Dog vaccination schedule	3
Favorites	4
Daily routine	4 - 6
Worm control	7 - 8
Medical & surgical history	9 - 13
Vaccination	14 - 18
Grooming history	19 - 23
Memorable events	24 - 26
Dog language	27

Pet details

Pet name   ....

Date of birth   ....

Species / Breed ....

Sex M/F   ....

Microchip / Special markings ....

Color   ....

Pet parent details

Name   ....

Address   ....

                ....

Phone | Mobile ....

Dog vaccination schedule

Puppy's Age	Recommended Vaccinations
6 - 7 weeks	Distemper, Parvovirus
9 - 10 weeks	DHPPL (vaccines for Distemper, Leptospira, Adenovirus [hepatitis], Parainfluenza, and Parvovirus)
12 - 14 weeks	DHPPL, Rabies
16 weeks	Rabies
Annual revaccination	DHPPL, Rabies

Keep me
Healthy !

KEEP ME VACCINATED

Favorite foods :

Favorite activities:

Accessories :

Daily routine

Day	Time	Activities

Daily routine

Day	Time	Activities

Daily routine

Day	Time	Activities

Date	Age	Weight	Comments

Date	Age	Weight	Comments

Date	Age	Weight	Comments

Date	Age	Weight	Comments

Date	Age	Weight	Comments

Date	Age	Weight	Comments

Date	Age	Weight	Comments

Vaccination

Date	Vaccine label	Due date	Signature & stamp of veterinarian

Vaccination

Date	Vaccine label	Due date	Signature & stamp of veterinarian

Vaccination

Date	Vaccine label	Due date	Signature & stamp of veterinarian

Date	Vaccine label	Due date	Signature & stamp of veterinarian

Vaccination

Date	Vaccine label	Due date	Signature & stamp of veterinarian

Date	Grooming type	Comments

Date	Grooming type	Comments

Date	Grooming type	Comments

Date	Grooming type	Comments

Date	Grooming type	Comments

Date	Event

Date	Event

Date	Event

DOGGIE LANGUAGE

starring Boogie the Boston Terrier

ALERT

SUSPICIOUS

ANXIOUS

THREATENED

ANGRY

"PEACE!"
look away/head turn

STRESSED
yawn

STRESSED
nose lick

"PEACE!"
sniff ground

"RESPECT!"
turn & walk away

"NEED SPACE"
whale eye

STALKING

STRESSED
scratching

STRESS RELEASE
shake off

RELAXED
soft ears, blinky eyes

"RESPECT!"
offer his back

FRIENDLY & POLITE
curved body

FRIENDLY

"PRETTY PLEASE"
round puppy face

"I'M YOUR LOVEBUG"
belly-rub pose

"HELLO I LOVE YOU!"
greeting stretch

"I'M FRIENDLY!"
play bow

"READY!"
prey bow

"YOU WILL FEED ME"

CURIOUS
head tilt

HAPPY
(or hot)

OVERJOYED
wiggly

"MMMM...."

"I LOVE YOU,
DON'T STOP"